Behind

The Flying

You'd be amazed what lies behind the Flying Ducks name.

Flying Ducks Publications and **The Flying Ducks Theatre Company** write, publish and produce comedy plays which fly all over the world.

Our **Live Events** wing stages conferences, gala dinners and roadshows at home and abroad, for some of the country's best-known businesses.

Our **Multimedia** wing produces video programmes, devises multimedia presentations for use on cd-rom, touchscreen and dvd, and designs web sites for companies large and small.

Our **Computer Services** wing designs and installs network computer systems and provides IT training.

And **Flying Ducks Facilities** hires audio-visual equipment and crew, and we have superb broadcast standard video facilities for shooting, editing, encoding and duplicating - all here at Duck HQ.

If, when you're not treading the boards, you'd like us to help your business fly, check out our web site, or call us on 01785 610966.

www.**flyingducks.biz**

A Flying Ducks Publication

NOTES PAGE

A Flying Ducks Publication

The story so far...

The Little Grimley sagas have become a modern-day theatrical phenomenon. Rarely have one-act plays been gobbled up with such relish by amateur societies all over the world.

It started with **Last Tango**, in which our four heroes battled to save their ailing am-dram with a home-grown sex comedy. It turned into an evening the locals would only forget after years of expensive counselling.

Then came **Last Panto**, in which the prolific Gordon unveiled the world's greatest pantomime ("Oh, no it wasn't!")

And now, the querulous quartet finally try to tackle a musical – traditionally their Achilles heel. Well, one of their many Achilles heels, to be fair. This is a society with more weak heels than a lame centipede.

The odds are stacked against them – not just stacked, but piled to the rafters, higher than a giant's supermarket shelf in a clearance sale. The locals who saw their last production are still in therapy and suing for psychological damage. What's more, a rival society – and a very good one too – has set up on their doorstep, and is selling tickets like hot cakes. And they're performing the same musical.

It all looks a little grim for Little Grimley. But it's never over...until the Fat Lady sings.

A Flying Ducks Publication

Other Plays by David Tristram

ONE-ACT

Last Tango in Little Grimley
Last Panto in Little Grimley
Joining the Club
Brenton versus Brenton
A Jolly Sinister Jape
The Extraordinary Revelations of Orca the Goldfish
What's For Pudding?

FULL-LENGTH

The Opposite Sex
Unoriginal Sin
Inspector Drake's Last Case
Inspector Drake and the Time Machine
Inspector Drake and the Perfekt Crime
The Secret Lives of Henry & Alice
Cinders – the True Story
Ghost Writer
Forget-Me-Knot
Sex, Drugs & Rick'n'Noel

You'll find more details on all the plays, including synopses, extracts and acting editions for sale on the web site:
www.flyingducks.biz

A Flying Ducks Publication

THE FAT LADY SINGS
IN LITTLE GRIMLEY

A comedy by David Tristram

A Flying Ducks Publication

NOTES PAGE

Characters
(in order of their own sense of self-importance)

Gordon

Margaret

Joyce

Bernard

A Flying Ducks Publication

PERFORMING LICENCES

Rights of performance by Amateurs and Professionals are controlled by Samuel French Limited, 52, Fitzroy Street, London W1T 5JR.

Samuel French, or their authorized agents, issue licences on payment of a fee.

It is an infringement of the Copyright to give any performance or public reading of this play before the fee has been paid and the licence issued.

The publication of this play does not imply that it is necessarily available for performance by Amateurs or Professionals, either in the British Isles or Overseas.

Amateurs and Professionals considering a production are strongly advised, in their own interests, to apply to Samuel French, or their overseas agents, for consent before starting rehearsals or booking a theatre or hall.

VIDEO RECORDING OF AMATEUR PRODUCTIONS

Please note that the copyright laws governing video recording are extremely complex and that it should not be assumed that any play may be video recorded for whatever purpose without first obtaining the permission of the appropriate agents. The fact that a play is published does not indicate that video rights are available or that Samuel French control such rights.

For more information on Flying Ducks Publications, check the web site.

www.flyingducks.biz

ISBN 1 900997 05 3

A Flying Ducks Publication

THE FAT LADY SINGS
In Little Grimley

We begin with one of the tensest and longest silences in theatrical history. The lights fade up to reveal four chairs – one empty, the other three occupied by Gordon, Margaret and Joyce. From their body language, it's clear there's been some kind of major disagreement. Gordon is fuming. Joyce has a look of stubborn defiance. Margaret seems exasperated by the other two. Finally, after a major psychological battle of wills and several false starts, Gordon cracks and barks an apology at Joyce.

Gordon: All right I'm sorry!
Margaret: Thank Christ for that. Joyce?
Joyce: *(triumphantly)* Apology accepted.
Gordon: Can we possibly get on now?
Joyce: All he had to do was apologise.
Margaret: Well he has, Joyce, so let's just put it behind us.
Gordon: She takes offence too easily.
Margaret: Gordon, you called her a talentless moron.
Gordon: But why take it so personally?
Margaret: Can we just get through the agenda? I told Ryan I'd be back no later than nine. He's cooking me a romantic meal for two.
Joyce: Oh! What's the special occasion?
Margaret: It's his turn. I collected the pizza yesterday.
Gordon: Where's Bernard?
Margaret: We can't wait any longer, Gordon. Agenda, come on.
Gordon: But it's the last meeting before the AGM, Margaret – we need a good turn out.
Margaret: Agenda, Gordon, now, or I'm off.
Gordon: All right, I'm calling the meeting to order. Item one…what are you scribbling at, Joyce?
Joyce: I'm taking the minutes, Gordon.
Gordon: We haven't started yet.
Joyce: Yes we have – item one on the agenda – Apologies.
Gordon: And what have you written?
Joyce: I've written "Gordon, to Joyce - eventually".
Gordon: Why?
Joyce: Because that was the first apology.
Gordon: No, Joyce. That is not an apology.
Joyce: Oh, is it not indeed!
Margaret: On a meeting agenda, Joyce, apologies does not mean apologies. It means people who aren't here. People apologise for not being here.
Joyce: How can people apologise if they're not here?

Margaret: They just do, Joyce, it's a convention.

Joyce: So where do I minute the fact that Gordon has apologised to me?

Gordon: You don't, Joyce – that was before the meeting started.

Joyce: I'm sorry, Gordon, but I insist on officially minuting the fact that you apologised to me.

Gordon: Not under apologies you don't.

Joyce: Where then?

Margaret: Put it under 'Any Other Business', Joyce. Item four.

Joyce: Gordon?

Gordon: Whatever, let's just get on with it.

Joyce: Right. So what do I write under apologies?

Gordon: How many of us are there in this society, Joyce?

Joyce: Four.

Gordon: And how many of us are here?

Joyce: Three.

Gordon: That, Joyce, is the raw data you need to complete the apologies section of the minutes.

Joyce: What does he mean?

Gordon: Bloody hell, save me from this woman.

Margaret: Who's not here, Joyce?

Joyce: Bernard.

Enter Bernard.

Bernard: Sorry – M6 was a bloody nightmare. Have I missed anything?

Gordon: Just the apologies, Bernard.

Bernard: Oh – who's apologised for what?

Gordon: You have, Bernard, for not being here.

Margaret: And Gordon has, to Joyce, for calling her a moron.

Bernard: A moron? He's obviously warming to you, Joyce.

Gordon: Sit down, Bernard - we've got a lot to get through.

Margaret: And I have to be away by quarter to. Ryan is cooking me a... *(Bernard unceremoniously bites into a banana)* ...never mind.

Joyce: So, now that Bernard's apologised for not being here – is he an apology or not?

Gordon: No, Joyce. Because he's here.

Joyce: But he did say sorry...

Gordon: Just leave it, Joyce! He's here – all right? Look – Bernard, banana, banana, Bernard - that's all you need to know!

A bemused pause.

Joyce: *(pointing to the minutes)* So...

Gordon: *(ranting furiously) Nothing,* Joyce! You write nothing! Everybody's here! Just write nothing at all. Stop writing. No apologies. Don't put anything. *(Joyce hastily scribbles a note)* What the f...what's she doing! The woman's insane!

Joyce hands the note to Margaret.

Margaret: *(reading the note)* Joyce isn't talking to you for the rest of the evening, Gordon, because you're a vile bully.
Gordon: Tell her I'm gutted, Margaret.
Margaret: Gordon says he's...
Joyce: I can hear him, Margaret.
Margaret: She can hear you, Gordon.
Gordon: I know she can hear me, Margaret!
Margaret: No need to shoot the messenger, Gordon.
Gordon: All right – everybody just...calm down.
Margaret: Huh! Physician, heal thyself.
Gordon: May I continue?

Joyce mutters something to Margaret about the minutes.

Margaret: *(confidentially)* Just write "no apologies". *(Joyce looks bewildered)* Honestly. And cross out the bit about the banana.

Gordon finally silences them with a withering stare, like two naughty children in a classroom.

Gordon: Thank you. Right – item two on the agenda. The rent. It needs paying. And we haven't got any money.
Margaret: No problem.
Gordon: Oh, you don't consider that problematic, Margaret?
Margaret: No more so than normal. You know perfectly well we can fund our debts with the proceeds of our next production.
Gordon: Which is what?
Margaret: Which is item three on the agenda.
Gordon: And it's a simple as that, is it?
Margaret: Yes. Why do Chairmen always have to over-dramatize everything?
Gordon: Would the Treasurer kindly inform the rest of the committee of the nature of our financial predicament.
Margaret: Joyce isn't talking to you, Gordon.
Gordon: Margaret, kindly inform the Treasurer to kindly inform the rest of the committee of the nature of our financial predicament.
Margaret: Joyce, kindly inform...
Joyce: I heard him. *(She coughs, and produces a letter)* As of last week, our funds

are in the red to the tune of £287 and nine pence.

Margaret: What?

Bernard: What happened to all the panto money?

Gordon: The panto is the reason we're in so much debt, Bernard. We spent £150 on staging...

Margaret: Yes, and we took nearly £600 on advance ticket sales!

Gordon: Correct Margaret. Making a profit of approximately £450. So far so good. Then, we then made the fatal error. We decided to actually perform the pantomime in front of a live audience. And?

Margaret: Okay, so a small proportion of the populace found it controversial – you get this with all great art, Gordon.

Bernard: I thought it went quite well.

Gordon: By what measure, Bernard?

Bernard: Well, we got through the bugger, didn't we? That's more than we ever did in rehearsals.

Gordon: Yes, we got through the bugger, Bernard. No argument there. And afterwards, a total of 84 members of the audience who also "got through the bugger" wrote to me and asked for their money back. This I duly did, for the sake of community harmony. But the scars obviously run deep. No less than seven members of the public have since taken things a stage further. In fact, they've banded together to engage the services of a solicitor, who's now suing us for psychological damage. Thanks to the pantomime, we are now facing financial ruin on a scale not seen since, well, since our previous production.

Margaret: Never mind the finances. What about our reputation?

Gordon: That remains unaffected, Margaret.

Bernard: Okay, so this year's panto was a bit iffy. No big deal, we can make it up.

Gordon: How, Bernard?

Bernard: Well, how about we just put up our ticket prices next time.

Gordon: Interesting tactic, Bernard. So we torture innocent members of the public to the limits of their sanity, put them through unbearable psychological trauma, and then tell them that, if they wish to come back again, it will cost them more.

Margaret: You really do exaggerate, Gordon.

Gordon: Facts, Margaret. All the research we've done in the past has shown us that when tickets prices get above a certain level, sales start tailing off.

Bernard: What bloody research?

Gordon: Well, for example, three years ago we charged £1.20 for the tickets. We sold 8. Then the following year we put the price up to £1.25. And nobody bought any.

Margaret: Correction, Gordon.

Gordon: All right, Margaret, Ryan bought one. But only as a birthday present for your mother.

Bernard: Ryan wouldn't do that – he hates your mother.

Gordon: Precisely, Bernard.

Bernard: Oh. What about kids?

Gordon: What about them?

Bernard: Well, that's an age-old trick isn't it? Stick loads of kids in your show, then they all bring their aunties, uncles, grannies and things. Instant sell-out.

Gordon: I looked at that last year. I invited the local Brownie pack to take part in our panto.

Margaret: And?

Gordon: They sent a scout to see one of our rehearsals. He reported back. I then got a letter on official Brownie notepaper.

Margaret: And?

Gordon: It said we fell below their minimum standards.

Margaret: The Brownies blew us out?

Gordon: Yes.

Margaret: Cheeky blighters. I'll give them what for next time they offer to clean my windows. Bob-A-Job indeed.

Joyce: That's the cubs, Margaret.

Margaret: Same thing. Bloody Baden Powell and his woggle brigade. If you ask me they all want stringing up by their gin-gan goolies.

Gordon: So? Any suggestions for a sure-fire hit?

Bernard: I still say the panto drags 'em in.

Gordon: Not in August, Bernard. And not with law suits still pending. Margaret?

Margaret: Comedy every time.

Gordon: *(sourly)* Hah!

Bernard: That's the biggest laugh we've ever had.

Gordon: Joyce?

Margaret: Joyce isn't...

Gordon: Yes, I'm sorry, I forgot, Joyce isn't talking to me, is she. Still, never mind. I think we all know where Joyce's allegiance lies, don't we? She's still clinging to the pathetic idea that we can tackle a bloody musical.

Margaret: Your name may be Gordon, Gordon, but this is not Hell's Kitchen. Kindly keep a civil tongue in your head.

Gordon: Just ask her.

Margaret: Is that right, Joyce?

Joyce: No-one has ever given me a sensible reason why we shouldn't tackle a musical.

Gordon: Joyce, the last time we did a musical there were complaints from the neighbouring alley cats.

Joyce: Oh, it's very easy to pick faults, isn't it, Gordon.

Gordon: With us, Joyce – yes, it is.

Joyce gets out an old programme.

Joyce: Look. That's me, in 1987, in Hello Dolly. It was total sell-out.

A Flying Ducks Publication

Margaret: But the society was bigger in those days, Joyce. It had members and things. I mean, look – look at all these people - it's not just singers, you need musicians. I can't play anything.

Joyce: Well I can, Margaret.

Margaret: Oh? What can you play, Joyce?

Joyce: I had lessons when I was young. I was told I was very gifted.

Gordon: What can you play, Joyce?

Margaret: Stay out of this, Gordon. What can you play, Joyce?

Joyce: I don't want to say. You'll just try and ridicule me.

Margaret: No we wouldn't, Joyce. Would we, Gordon?

Gordon: Try me.

Margaret: Pay no attention to him, Joyce. I didn't know you had hidden talents.

Bernard: Bloody well hidden.

Margaret: Shut it, Bernard. Joyce?

A tense pause.

Joyce: The banjo.

Gordon: Hah!

Joyce: There is nothing wrong with the banjo, Gordon.

Gordon: No, Joyce, it's a fine and noble instrument. I would have gone for it myself at school but, well, you know how it is with kids – the banjo course was completely over-subscribed.

Bernard: I had a crack at the trombone when I was a kid. School brass band. Still got the bugger somewhere.

Margaret: I thought you'd never be far from a U-bend.

Bernard: What?

Gordon: Fantastic thought, eh? Songs from the shows. Hum along to all your favourite melodies, accompanied by Joyce and Bernard on banjo and trombone.

Bernard: What's she mean, U-bend?

Joyce: I'd like to make a suggestion…

Gordon: Right, if there are no meaningful suggestions, allow me to move onto item four on the agenda…

Margaret: We haven't decided item three yet. What about our next production?

Gordon: We don't need one, Margaret.

Margaret: What do you mean?

Gordon: I was just going through the motions, Margaret, for the sake of good old democracy. But in fact, I needn't have wasted my breath. Because item four is 'Any Other Business'. And all you need to minute here, Joyce, is three simple words. We're…all…doomed.

Margaret: Meaning?

Gordon: Meaning, Margaret, this.

Margaret: What's that?

Gordon: It's a poster.
Margaret: I can see that, Gordon. What's it for?
Gordon: It's a poster for the opening production of the new amateur dramatic society here in Grimley.

A stunned silence.

Bernard: What?
Gordon: Let me spell it out for you, Bernard. The village has a new amateur dramatic society.
Others: No!
Gordon: Yes!

Another stunned pause.

Others: No!!
Gordon: Yes!!
Margaret: Little Grimley has a new amateur society?
Gordon: Well, near enough. Grimley-Upon-Neenton.
Margaret: Aha!
Gordon: What do you mean, "Aha!"?
Margaret: Grimley-Upon-Neenton is not Little Grimley, Gordon.
Gordon: It is, near as dammit.
Margaret: Oh, no it isn't.
Bernard: Oh, yes it is!
Margaret: Oh, no it...shut up, Bernard. The two communities have very distinctive personalities, Gordon. People simply will not travel.
Gordon: It's two miles, Margaret.
Margaret: No matter. Little Grimley is extremely parochial. Trust me, I know these things. The villagers won't buy it.
Gordon: They've already bought it, Margaret. It's a complete sell-out.
Margaret: *(snatching the poster from him and examining it)* What? Give me that! Grimley-Upon-Neenton Amateur Dramatic Society. GUNADS. Well I say.
Joyce: What are they doing?
Bernard: *(snatching the poster)* "Sex, Drugs and Rick'n'Noel."
Margaret: Sounds absolutely ghastly.
Gordon: It's a new musical by David Tristram.
Joyce: A musical!
Gordon: Yes, Joyce, it's a musical. And it's got the word sex in it. A sure-fire winner.
Bernard: *(he says something totally indistinguishable, courtesy of another banana)*
Gordon: Joyce, would you like to minute that?

Joyce looks flustered.

Margaret: Bernard, do you have to behave like some sort of half-starved primary ape?

Bernard: Shag off, you poncy tart.

Margaret: Did you ever consider a career in the clergy, Bernard?

Gordon: What was it exactly that you wished to contribute to the debate, Bernard?

Bernard: I was just saying, if they've set up a rival am-dram next door, and they're doing a musical, and it's got sex in the title, all in all, I reckon we're bolloxed.

Gordon: So, you reckon we're "bolloxed".

Bernard: Yep. Totally.

Gordon: And does everyone else agree with Bernard's clinical analysis of our dilemma? Joyce?

Margaret: Joyce isn't talking to you, Gordon.

Gordon: Pity – that our little discussion should be cruelly robbed of such an intellect. Margaret?

Margaret: Well, admittedly, having a rival society in our midst may have a temporarily adverse affect on our revenue streams.

Bernard: What's that mean?

Margaret: It means we're completely bolloxed. *(Sudden lapse into panic)* These people are going to steal our audiences, Gordon.

Gordon: Margaret, we haven't got any audiences.

Margaret: We have a loyal core.

Gordon: That's not a core, Margaret – it's a pip. And it's not so loyal.

Bernard: Oh, I don't know. Year in, year out, rain or shine, hell or high water, the bastards stay away.

Margaret: Well, it's despicable. Who's behind this?

Gordon: *(looking flustered)* Erm, a lady returning to the village after a spell of absence – ex-pro actress. Very good, by all accounts.

Margaret: Ex-pro actress indeed. I bet she did one toothpaste commercial in the fifties.

Gordon: No, trod the boards with the best of them, apparently. Caused quite a stir when she was younger.

Margaret: And how do you know so much about her?

Gordon: Because, Margaret – it's Miriam.

A stunned silence.

Margaret: Oh, Gordon – not Miriam?

Gordon: Yes, Margaret. Miriam. She's come back. Back, to haunt me. Back, to… *(his voice trembles)* Excuse me. I need some air.

Exit Gordon.

Margaret: *(walking dramatically off to the side)* Oh, my God! Miriam's back!
Bernard: *(shocked, head in hands)* Oh, my God!
Joyce: Oh, no! *(looking initially shocked in sympathy with the others, but also bewildered, she eventually plucks up courage to whisper to Bernard)* Who's Miriam?
Bernard: Haven't got a clue.
Margaret: Miriam is Gordon's ex-wife.
Joyce: Oh! I never knew!
Margaret: Oh, yes.
Bernard: How long's Gordon had an ex-wife?
Margaret: Ever since she divorced him. Must be twenty years ago now. She ran off with Gordon's leading man. Very acrimonious.
Joyce: How do you spell that?
Margaret: No, you're not to minute this, Joyce. Gordon was severely scarred by the whole wretched experience. Poor lamb. No wonder he's been so bad-tempered and edgy tonight.
Bernard: Oh. I just put it down to the fact that he's always bad-tempered and edgy.
Margaret: Well, now we know. Miriam might just as well have torn open Gordon's shirt and driven a stake into his heart.
Bernard: Why – is he a vampire?
Margaret: Joyce, I think you should apologise to Gordon for taking offence when he called you a moron.
Joyce: I'm sorry.
Margaret: No, not to me. Gordon is clearly at the absolute split-end of his emotional tether. He desperately, desperately needs our support.
Bernard: Desperately.
Margaret: Are you taking the piss, Bernard?
Bernard: Desperately.
Margaret: Well…shhh, he's coming back.

Gordon enters, pale and drained.

Gordon: I'm sorry.
Margaret: Don't be. We all understand. Don't we, Bernard?
Bernard: Desperately.
Margaret: Even Joyce understands, don't you Joyce?
Joyce: Yes, Gordon. And I want to apologise.
Gordon: What for, Joyce?
Joyce: For being called a moron. It was stupid of me.
Gordon: Oh, I wouldn't have you any other way, Joyce.
Joyce: Thank you, Gordon.
Gordon: No, thank you, Joyce. All of you. I know that, well, we've had our

differences in the past – petty squabbles, minor disagreements, the occasional major disagreement, isolated outbursts of physical violence – but I've never forgotten that, despite everything, you three have always been there. God knows, it hasn't always been easy. In fact, I would go so far as to say, it's never been easy. But we were a team – a family, of sorts. And you all stuck by me, through thick... *(he glances at Joyce)* through thick, and thin. Anyway, despite all your touching shows of loyalty, the facts remain – everything that Bernard said earlier was true. A rival society in our midst, the return of Miriam, a new musical with 'Sex' in the title – I think deep down, we all know what it means.

Bernard/Margaret/Joyce: We're bolloxed.
Gordon: Precisely. I'm afraid...it's over.

They all hang their heads. The silence is broken by a defiant Margaret.

Margaret: *(very dramatically)* It's never over, until the fat lady sings.
Gordon: Sorry?
Margaret: Give Joyce a chance to sing, Gordon - before we disband. *(Joyce looks nonplussed)* Please. You know it's been her life's dream.
Joyce: Is she saying I'm fat?
Bernard: Only on the surface, Joyce.
Margaret: It's just an expression, Joyce. You've always said we should do a musical. For all we know you could be right. It could have been our salvation. And we never put it to the test.
Gordon: Margaret...
Margaret: This new Tristram musical. Sex, Drugs and whatsits. How many are in the cast?
Gordon: Please, Margaret...
Margaret: How many, Gordon?
Gordon: This isn't fair.
Margaret: How many, Gordon?
Gordon: Don't go there, Margaret.
Margaret: We could do it, couldn't we?
Gordon: No!
Margaret: How many, Gordon!
Gordon: *(reluctantly)* Two male and two female. *(The others exchange glances)* But that doesn't mean...
Margaret: Gordon! You promised Joyce.
Gordon: Did I?
Margaret: Yes.
Gordon: When?
Margaret: Every week for the last twelve years. "One day, Joyce," you said. "One day." Well, I think that day has finally come. After all - what have we got to lose?
Gordon: The remaining shreds of our dignity, Margaret. I'm sorry, Joyce. Even

under normal circumstances a musical would be challenging. But look what we're up against. A rival production - a good one - on our own doorstep. The odds are too great. I'm sorry. I'm disbanding the society.

Gordon collects his coat and walks slowly away. Joyce dissolves into tears, comforted by Margaret.

Bernard: Woh! Hang on a minute. There's an old saying, right. All's fair in love and war. Well, the way I see it from this side of the fence, Gordon here's been a bit short-changed in the old love department. His missus running off with the leading man – not exactly playing the game to the rules, is it? So, level playing field – game of two halves. Let's put the boot on the other foot for a minute. Love and war, eye for an eye – who's up for raising the stakes to balance the books?

A perplexed silence from the others.

Gordon: What?
Bernard: Eh?
Margaret: What did that bag of old clichés actually mean, Bernard?
Bernard: It means – let's not take this lying down, it's time to stand up and be counted. Look - there's a couple of geezers I met when I was in the East End – nice chaps, but, you know, hard – if you follow my drift.
Gordon: I think so.
Bernard: Anyway, they've set up this new business. They call themselves "The Persuaders." Now, I reckon…
Gordon: Bernard, are you suggesting what I think you're suggesting?
Bernard: Depends what you think I'm suggesting.
Gordon: You know what I think you're suggesting.
Bernard: In that case, probably.
Margaret: Would you two mind conducting the rest of this conversation in English?
Gordon: Bernard is suggesting that his two East End friends give my ex-wife what they would no doubt term 'a bit of a slap.'
Margaret: Bernard!
Bernard: No, nothing heavy – just enough to put the frighteners on a bit.
Gordon: Bernard, this woman once shared my house. She was mother to my children. We had seven glorious years together. No matter what has passed between us since, I cannot countenance violence towards her.
Bernard: What about the leading man?
Gordon: That's different – let's nobble him.
Bernard: Right, well, it just so happens, I've downloaded their rate card off the internet. I needed it last week to squeeze a landlord who wouldn't pay his plastering bill. What do you fancy? They do a broken collar bone and serious bruising for a hundred and fifty notes. Or how about this one - the brown underpants introductory

offer – no violence – just put the frighteners on – seventy quid. All prices are plus VAT, by the way.

Margaret: These people charge VAT?

Bernard: Oh, yeah, they're quite legit. They got a new starter grant from the Government. Here, look here's a good offer, if you collect three of these vouchers, they'll do you a broken leg for a pony.

Joyce: Oh, that's cruel!

Bernard: What?

Joyce: Breaking a pony's leg.

Gordon: No Joyce, a pony's a cockney expression. It means twenty-five pounds.

Margaret: When you two have finished your ridiculous macho ritual, can we get back into the real world. I have a better idea. Let's hit them where it hurts.

Bernard: They do that as well – fifteen quid plus VAT.

Margaret: I'm not talking about physical violence, Bernard. I'm talking about bruising them psychologically.

Gordon: Meaning?

Margaret: We won't nobble them, we'll nobble their production.

Gordon: Interesting. How do we do that?

Margaret: Plenty of ways.

Gordon: Such as?

Margaret: Steal the props.

Joyce: Or the costumes.

Bernard: I know, we could infiltrate their production and act in it.

Margaret: Bernard!

Bernard: Joyce could even sing.

Joyce: Bernard!

Gordon: All right, all right. Forget sabotage. Security's too tight. Their front of house manager is a gentleman – and I use the term advisedly – by the name of Spike Henderson, an ex-bouncer from the Dog and Donkey. He makes Bernard's East End friends look like pussy cats. Trust me - you'd never get near the place.

Margaret: Okay, if we can't nobble them, and we can't nobble their production, let's nobble their audience.

Gordon: Explain.

Margaret: Where's their box office?

Gordon: Mrs Miggins' sweet shop in Grimley.

Margaret: Mmm, Mrs Miggins, eh?

Gordon: What are you scheming, Margaret?

Margaret: If I know the meticulous Mrs Miggins, she will have logged the phone number of everyone who bought a ticket.

Gordon: And…

Margaret: I dare say that, with a little subterfuge, I could get hold of those phone numbers.

Gordon: And…

Margaret: I dare say I could call everyone on the list, saying that the production, due to circumstances beyond our control, unfortunately has had to be...cancelled.
Joyce: Margaret!
Bernard: That's brilliant!
Joyce: You've cracked it.
Margaret: Thank you.
Gordon: No.
Margaret: What?
Gordon: I said no, Margaret.
Margaret: You don't like the idea?
Gordon: Like it? I love it. But the production should not be cancelled. Merely...moved to a different venue.
Joyce: You don't mean?
Gordon: Yes, Joyce. Our musical...is on.

Dramatic military percussive music links the scenes. As the lights fade back up, Gordon is addressing the other three in a military style briefing, pointing with a stick and using a flip chart, or slides, showing the relevant photographs, maps, etc.

Gordon: *(pointing to a photo)* George Walker. Leading man and wife stealer. If Plan A goes pear-shaped, he's your prime target, Bernard.
Bernard: Consider him nobbled.
Gordon: *(pointing to another picture)* Harry Henderson. Also known as Spike. He'll be arranging security for the stage door *(switching to a diagram)* - here - and front of house cover for the main entrances - here, here, and here. Now, be in no doubt - these people are professional and well-drilled. On opening night, they'll be ready for a full house *(flipping to a map and pointing)* here, at the Village Hall, Grimley-Upon-Neenton. And they'll have every angle covered. Programme sales, tea and scones, raffle tickets, the works. They'll even know their lines. *(A shocked intake of breath and murmurings from the others)* But, what they won't be expecting, is for the entire audience to be two miles away - here, in the Village Hall at Little Grimley. Now this all depends on the success of the most important phase - Operation Sweet Shop. Margaret - that's where you come in.
Margaret: *(standing)* I'll need a diversion. I'll go in first and ask to buy a ticket. Mrs Miggins will tell me it's sold out. I'll remonstrate, and she's bound to reveal where all the paperwork is kept while she proves her point, or checks for any cancellations. Joyce - that's your cue. I need you to burst in, in a hurry, and ask for some of those lemon bon-bons - you know, the ones she keeps high on the back shelf...
Gordon: Hang on, hang on – this involves acting?
Margaret: Just asking for sweets.
Gordon: *(thoughtfully)* Yeah, okay.
Margaret: Right, Joyce - when Mrs Miggins' back is turned I'll grab the list.

Bernard, you come in behind me - I'll slip you the list, and you leg it to the local library for a photostat while I keep Mrs Miggins talking.

Bernard: That's a good ten minutes away.

Margaret: So?

Bernard: Are you going to be able to keep her talking for that long?

Margaret: *(flatly, as if it were a daft question)* Yes. Now, when Bernard returns, he asks for another half a pound of bon-bons, and I'll return the list. She'll never know she's been hustled.

Gordon: Any questions?

Joyce: What do I do with the lemon bon-bons?

Gordon: Eat them, Joyce.

Joyce: What about my figure?

Gordon: It's never over Joyce, till the fat lady sings. Right – any questions?

Bernard/Margaret: No.

Gordon: All right. Synchronise watches. It's Thursday. We meet back here next Thursday, 7pm sharp. And remember - it's top security on this one. If any of you are caught, I'll have to deny all knowledge of you. Good luck.

Military music again to end the scene. Lights up to reveal Margaret on a mobile phone. The others are listening anxiously.

Margaret: Oh, Mrs Thompson, yes – it's just about the musical next week...yes, that's the one, well, I'm afraid we've had to move it to another venue. Yes. It's now at the Village Hall in Little Grimley. Oh, good. All right. Yes, isn't it! Thank you! *(Crossing a name from a list)* That's the last one.

An excited cheer from the others.

Gordon: So, in precisely six days and...*(they all simultaneously check their watches)* seventeen minutes, Grimley-Upon-Neenton ADS will be set up in their Village Hall – smugly gloating over their sold-out stickers – and no-one shows up.

Margaret: I love it!

Bernard: A real kick in the GUNADS.

Gordon: Nicely put, Bernard. And here's the best bit. While they're scratching their heads wondering what's happened to their audience, we'll be packing them to the rafters.

Joyce: *(excitedly clapping)* Oh, Gordon! How many?

Gordon: Two hundred and fifty, Joyce. Two hundred and fifty people – all buzzing with excitement, and all coming to watch *our* production. *(There are big grins all round, then a moment's thought. The grins freeze into a look of total panic).* Shit! We haven't got a production.

Margaret: We've been so wrapped up in trying to scuttle their show we forgot to do one of our own.

Joyce: What are we going to do?
Bernard: Don't panic. We've still got six days.
Margaret: And seventeen minutes.
Bernard/Joyce: *(checking their watches simultaneously)* Sixteen.
Gordon: Terrific. Let's take a break. I'd hate to peak too early.
Margaret: We have to cancel.
Gordon: After all this? Do you realise how stupid we're going to look if we pull out now?
Margaret: And just how stupid are we going to look if we put on a show with less than a week's preparation?

The others glance at each other, then shrug out an answer.

Others: About normal.
Margaret: This is madness – I'm out of here.
Gordon: Margaret! Your fingerprints are all over this. Every single member of the audience will be able to trace this production directly back to your mobile. You walk out now, and you'll never be able to show your face in this village again.
Margaret: *(sexually charged)* You're a hard man.
Gordon: Harder than you'll ever know.
Joyce: Oh, Gordon – what's to become of us?
Gordon: Don't worry. I have a detailed strategy already worked out.
Margaret: You do?
Gordon: Yes. I'm going to the pub. And I'm going to get extremely drunk.
Bernard: *(following him)* Count me in.
Gordon: *(stopping and turning)* Meet me back here in twenty-four hours.

They again check watches simultaneously. Exit Gordon and Bernard.

Joyce: He's magnificent when he's angry.

Lights to black. Music links to next scene. Bernard is trying to get a noise out of a trombone, much to the annoyance of Margaret and Joyce. There's no sign of Gordon.

Margaret: Bernard, you are testing my notoriously short patience.
Bernard: I used to be able to get a tune out of this bugger.
Margaret: Are you sure you're blowing from the right hole.
Bernard: *(examining it)* It's never been the same since the kids got hold of it.
Joyce: Twenty-four hours he said. Are you sure that meant tonight?
Margaret: Well that's the usual interpretation of the phrase, Joyce.
Joyce: Only, I went to that new Tesco last week, and it was shut.

A bemused look from the others.

A Flying Ducks Publication

Margaret: What are you talking about, Joyce?
Joyce: Well, they said it was open twenty-four hours. And it was shut. So I was wondering if it meant, it was open twenty-four hours, but not in a row.
Bernard: It's a strange world you live in, Joyce.

Gordon struts in triumphantly. He is smoking a cigar and clutching some A4 papers.

Gordon: Good evening, team.
Margaret: Is that a cigar, Gordon?
Gordon: This is a cigar, Margaret.
Margaret: Why are you smoking a cigar, Gordon?
Gordon: Because, Margaret – I'm celebrating.

He casually taps his cigar ash into the upturned bell end of Bernard's trombone.

Margaret: Celebrating what?
Gordon: The fact that I have cracked it.
Margaret: Cracked what?
Gordon: It, Margaret. *(He starts handing out scripts)*
Bernard: What's this?
Gordon: Our scripts. Get learning.
Margaret: But it's only one page long.
Gordon: Precisely. Rehearsal time is short and, therefore, so is the script.
Joyce: But what is it?
Gordon: The musical.
Bernard: What – all of it?
Gordon: Not exactly. I've précised it.
Margaret: You can't do that!
Gordon: I've done it, Margaret.
Margaret: It's against the law. The author would go mad.
Gordon: No he won't – he happens to be a close personal friend of mine.
Bernard: You know David Tristram?
Gordon: Yes.
Bernard: David Tristram the playwright?
Gordon: Yes.
Margaret: How?
Gordon: We were at school together.
Margaret: You went to the same school as David Tristram?
Gordon: I didn't say that. We were at school together. At the same time. They just happened to be different schools.
Margaret: Have you met him or not?
Gordon: Of course.

Margaret: When?
Gordon: Last night. I met him…in an email.
Margaret: Did he give you permission to change his script or not?
Gordon: *(nodding vaguely)* Mmm.
Margaret: That wasn't entirely convincing, Gordon.
Gordon: Trust me, Margaret. I have the permission I need.
Margaret: *(pushing him for clarity)* Gordon…
Gordon: I emailed him asking if we could present some extracts of his musical in an evening's entertainment, and he said yes. It just so happens that those extracts will be individual words from the script, re-arranged into a completely different order. And lasting a total of three minutes fifty-four seconds.
Margaret: Are you seriously suggesting that we invite a sell-out crowd here to witness three minutes of entertainment?
Gordon: Three minutes fifty-four seconds, Margaret. But I wouldn't guarantee it's all going to be entertaining. I've built in some light and shade.
Bernard: They'll go spare.
Gordon: Quite probably.
Margaret: And where does that leave us?
Gordon: Not us, Margaret – GUNADS. That's who they're coming to see, after all.
Bernard: So you're saying, we put on a pile of old cobblers, and blame it on the other lot?
Gordon: Precisely. After this, I imagine they'll view Little Grimley Amateur Dramatic Society as positively great value for money.
Joyce: But…they'll all want their money back.
Gordon: Quite right, Joyce. They will. And they can have it. From Mrs Miggins. The show was pre-sold. She holds all the funds.
Joyce: It'll ruin them.
Gordon: Yes.
Bernard: It'll be the end of their society.
Gordon: Yes.
Margaret: *(outraged)* But, this is…this is… *(a dawning smile)*…this is sheer genius.
Gordon: Yes. Scripts? *(They all obediently snatch their scripts into focus)* Right, Joyce, we start with a song. I'm afraid I've had to keep these fairly short as well. Lyrics are at the top of the page.
Joyce: Oh…what's the tune?
Gordon: Hit me with a note. *(Joyce warbles a note)* Right. Start there for the first two words, then go up a bit for the rest. *(Joyce looks bewildered)* Go on, try it.
Joyce: *(singing)* "This was a man…"
Gordon: Brilliant. Thank you, Joyce. Right Bernard, you're on.
Joyce: Is that it?
Gordon: Leave them wanting more, Joyce. Never a bad motto.
Joyce: But it was four words…
Gordon: Enough to set the scene, Joyce. "This was a man…" that's you, Bernard.

You play the leading man, Rick.

Bernard: The lead?

Gordon: Trust me. You'll cope. Now, the first four or five pages of the original script were like an extended monologue, where Rick introduces himself, tells us all about his background, and gives us a real insight into his later character - so I've had to cut that down a fair bit. Off you go, Bernard, from the top.

Bernard: "Hello".

Gordon: Perfect. You're on, Margaret.

Margaret: Who am I?

Gordon: You're Maxine Shepherd – Rick's University lecturer. They're quite wary of each other at first, but gradually they begin to get on really well and eventually fall in love. This is their opening scene.

Margaret: What's my motivation?

Gordon: Your motivation, Margaret, is the fact that we're putting this on in five days. Get on with it.

Margaret: "You must be Rick?"

Bernard: "Yes. And you must be Max, who I eventually fall in love with?"

Margaret: "Yes."

Gordon: Excellent. Now I'm on. I play Noel – a bit of a Jack the lad. Rick and Noel are like chalk and cheese to start with, but they become best buddies when they share a flat together. Okay Margaret – from my entrance.

Margaret: Er….

Gordon: Page one.

Margaret: Oh, right. "Rick – I'd like you to meet Noel."

Bernard: "Noel…"

Gordon: "Rick…"

Margaret: "Why don't you two share a flat together and have some adventures and then despite a dodgy start and apparent differences you can fairly predictably become great friends at the end?"

Bernard/Gordon: "Okay."

Gordon: Brilliant. Time for another song. Off you go, Bernard.

Bernard: Me?

Gordon: It's your character.

Bernard: I can't sing.

Gordon: I'm sure you can sing, Bernard. Remember, it doesn't need to be pleasant to listen to.

Bernard: No bloody way am I singing.

Gordon: Okay, *(snatching the trombone and thrusting it to him)* I'll settle for an instrumental version.

Bernard: Fair enough. What's the tune?

Gordon: Can you play this thing?

Bernard: No.

Gordon: Then it doesn't matter what the tune is, does it? Just blow.

Bernard blows for all he's worth. His eyes are popping. But to no avail.

Gordon: Harder. Come on, Bernard – give it some welly!

Bernard launches one final assault on the trombone. Suddenly, accompanied by a loud raspberry from the trombone, a dead hamster squirts out and lands at Joyce's feet. She screams and stands on a chair. Gordon picks it up by the tail.

Margaret: What the hell is it?
Gordon: Unless I'm hallucinating, I would say that it's a badly decomposed hamster.
Bernard: Bloody hell. So that's what happened to him.
Gordon: *(dropping the hamster unceremoniously back into the trombone)* Right. End of song. End of Act One. Off we go to the rapturous sound of dropping jaws.
Margaret: You're having an interval in a three minute play?
Gordon: We've got to make some money at this, Margaret – we need to do the raffle. All helps pay the rent. So – what do you think?
Margaret: Well, it's certainly concise.
Gordon: Yes, but despite all the cuts I reckon I've stayed faithful to the original text.
Bernard: I think I've learnt my lines already.
Gordon: There you go, then.
Joyce: Aren't there any more songs?
Gordon: Second half, Joyce. There were some more in the first half but I thought they were slowing down the action. Never mind. You open Act Two with a real belter. It's called "Under Control". That's the chorus hook line. Can't remember the tune – just have a go.
Joyce: *(trying to sing it with gusto based on an invented tune)* "Under Control... ...Under Control!"
Gordon: That's the idea. But because of time constraints I've shortened the title to just "Under".
Joyce: Under?
Gordon: Yes. Try it.
Joyce: *(trying to make sense of the disconnected and unresolved word)* "Under..."
Gordon: Lovely. I like that better. And that does away with the need for a proper tune. Okay, Joyce – tootle off and practise your songs, while we work on the scripts.
Joyce: Oh. But what about my acting?
Gordon: Acting?
Joyce: What part am I playing?
Gordon: Ah.
Joyce: I do have a part, don't I, Gordon?
Gordon: Not part, Joyce, parts. The script calls for a talented and versatile actress to play two roles - a student called Helen and also her twin sister Rachel. Helen and

Rachel – got it?
Joyce: Helen and Rachel. Right, Gordon. What are their characters?
Gordon: It doesn't matter, Joyce. As I hadn't got a talented and versatile actress available, I've cut both parts. And that brings us to the finale.
Margaret: Which is what?
Gordon: Which is too long, so I ditched it. And there you have it. A complete musical in under four minutes. So, shall we run it again, or do we think we've cracked it?
Bernard: It seems a shame to lose the spontaneity.
Gordon: Right, then. See you all back here on opening night. Don't be late, we've got a lot to pack in.

Margaret's mobile rings as they're leaving.

Margaret: Margaret Dumont? Yes? Who is this? I'm sorry, I'm in rehearsals at the moment. But...now just hold on a...how dare you talk to me like that...I... charming. Oh, dear.
Gordon: What?
Margaret: Only a matter of time, I suppose.
Joyce: What's the matter Margaret!?
Margaret: I think we may have a small problem.
Bernard: Who the bloody hell was it?!!!
Margaret: Spike Henderson. GUNADS' front of house manager.. They've found out what we're up to. He's on his way over here. Right now.

They all look at each other. Then scarper as the lights go to black. Music. Lights fade back up to reveal Joyce and Margaret. They are sitting in silence, staring forwards, deep in thought. Each is battered and bruised – black eyes, plasters, head bandages, arms in slings. Finally, Joyce breaks the melancholic silence.

Joyce: It went very well.
Margaret: It did.
Joyce: Audience loved it.
Margaret: Five minute standing ovation. Never seen anything like it.
Joyce: Stunning.
Margaret: Any news of Bernard?
Joyce: I spoke to his wife tonight. She said he's going to try and get here, if he can. But he didn't have a very comfortable night.
Margaret: Hardly surprising. I have to admit, he was very brave.
Joyce: I think he took the brunt of it.
Margaret: Mr Henderson doesn't take any prisoners, does he?
Joyce: I still can't get over Gordon.
Margaret: No. I was sickened to the pit of my stomach.

Joyce: Gordon, of all people.

Enter Bernard. One leg is in plaster, so he's using a crutch. His right arm is sticking straight out at 90 degrees to his body, because it's bandaged to a plank, and his trombone is bent around his neck.

Joyce: Hello, Bernard! How are you feeling?
Bernard: Sorry I'm late. I had to use the bus.
Margaret: Good of you to come, Bernard. We'd have understood if you didn't.
Bernard: Well, no good moping around the house. Never missed an AGM yet. No Gordon?
Margaret: That's a sore point.
Bernard: Oh, tell me later - I've got enough sore points for now. *(He sits awkwardly next to them. He is holding a banana in one hand, but can't get it near his mouth because the arm is stiff)* Joyce, would you mind?
Joyce: Of course. *(She takes the banana and feeds it to him)*
Margaret: What's the latest on the trombone, Bernard?
Bernard: They're going to let the swelling die down a bit, and then saw it off.
Margaret: Well, I suppose they know best.
Bernard: Yes.
Margaret: And erm…any news on the erm…*(confidentially)* the mouthpiece?
Bernard: I'm expecting that to show up any day now.
Margaret: Right.
Joyce: Keep taking the caster oil, Bernard. My mother swears by it.
Bernard: Sorry I missed the performance. What happened?
Margaret: Well, in a nutshell, after Mr Henderson had been dragged off by the police, those of us that could still talk and walk had a slightly more civilised meeting with GUNADS. They thought that it was too late to change venues again. So, they insisted on staging their musical here.
Bernard: And you let them?
Margaret: Let's just say they twisted my arm.
Bernard: So we didn't do our show?
Margaret: Well how could we? With our leading man in hospital?
Bernard: You could have cut my part – it was only fifteen words.
Joyce: I bet you'd learnt them as well.
Bernard: Most of them, yes.
Margaret: Not in the right order, surely?
Bernard: No. I normally leave that for dress rehearsals.
Margaret: Quite right.
Bernard: So, they beat us.
Margaret: Yes, Bernard, they beat us. Physically, morally, financially and, I'm afraid, artistically.
Joyce: Oh, Bernard – you should have seen it.

Bernard: What – you actually went?
Margaret: Well, I'm sorry, but curiosity got the better of us. We had to see what all the fuss was about. So Joyce and I decided to sneak in through the fire exit on the last night and watch from the back.
Bernard: And?
Margaret: And...though it grieves me to say it...it was absolutely stunning.
Joyce: Inspired.
Margaret: A five minute standing ovation.
Joyce: I cried.
Bernard: Terrific. What a way to bow out, eh. Battered into submission.
Margaret: Bruised egos.
Joyce: Bankrupt.
Bernard: And bolloxed.

A deep sigh from all.

Margaret: Do you know what hurts the most, Bernard?
Bernard: I think it's the left shin.
Margaret: No, I mean, emotionally.
Bernard: What?
Margaret: You tell him, Joyce – I can't bring myself to say the words.
Joyce: When Margaret and I came to see the show, we spotted Gordon.
Bernard: Well, he was probably just curious as well.
Joyce: He was a lot more than curious, Bernard. He was their new front of house manager.
Bernard: You're having me on.
Margaret: Oh, no. True as we're sitting here. Selling raffle tickets and programmes. Smiling and saying he hoped they all enjoyed the show.
Bernard: If I ever see him again I'll swing for him!

Gordon enters, with a black eye and his arm in a sling.

Gordon: Evening folks.
Joyce: Gordon!
Margaret: You've got a nerve showing up here.
Bernard: You bloody Judas!

Bernard has got up and is trying to swing kicks and punches at Gordon with whatever limbs he has left. Gordon is calmly keeping Bernard at bay by placing his hand on his brow and keeping him at arm's length.

Gordon: Calm down, Bernard, you'll do yourself an injury.
Joyce: We saw you, Gordon. We saw you – fraternalising with the enemy.

Gordon: I saw you too, Joyce. Hiding at the back of the room with Margaret.
Joyce: We were only curious – that's all.
Gordon: And I was only selling programmes, Joyce.
Margaret: And raffle tickets.
Gordon: Well, the raffle proceeds came to us, Margaret – £293 over the three nights. It's paid off our debts.
Margaret: Huh! Listen to him! Little Grimley's very own Man For All Seasons.
Gordon: What?
Margaret: I've heard of people selling their soul, Gordon, but you must be the first man who's ever raffled it off!
Joyce: How could you do it, Gordon?
Gordon: Well, we all have to get on in this world, Joyce. And as I was sitting in the queue at casualty, I started thinking, what with their front of house manager in gaol, perhaps they could do with a little help.
Bernard: Black leg!
Gordon: Black and blue, Bernard. I joined in the fighting too, remember.
Joyce: But that's what makes it so much harder to understand, Gordon.
Gordon: You two never bought a programme I notice.
Margaret: I never put my nose in the trough of my enemies, Gordon.
Gordon: Never mind, I've brought a few spares for you – as souvenirs.
Bernard: You know where you can shove your bloody souvenirs.
Gordon: *(producing some programmes)* Good, aren't they? From the outside, you wouldn't even know the difference.
Margaret: What do you mean – difference?
Gordon: Oh, didn't I mention it? I took the liberty of re-printing the inside sheets. Have a read.

He thrusts an opened copy under Bernard's nose.

Bernard: "Sex Drugs & Rick'n'Noel" the musical. Proudly brought to you by…Little Grimley Amateur Dramatic Society…"!

The others snatch the programme and start reading it.

Gordon: Yes, well - credits where credits are due, I thought. And something instinctively told me that their production wouldn't do our reputation any harm.
Joyce: Look! I'm the Musical Director!
Gordon: The least you deserve, Joyce.
Bernard: Set design by Bernard Collins!
Gordon: And a fabulous job you did of it, too, Bernard.
Margaret: Oh! Gordon! Did I really direct this masterpiece?
Gordon: Apparently so, Margaret.
Margaret: My God! I'm a genius.

Joyce: And look! Gordon wrote it!
Gordon: Yes. With a little help from an old school friend of mine.
Bernard: So…instead of us doing a crap show and blaming them…
Margaret: They do a magnificent show…
Joyce: And we take all the credit.
Gordon: Survival, ladies and gentlemen. It's all about adapting to the changing environment. Same plan – just in reverse. Oh, I even took the liberty of putting my phone number for advance bookings of our next show. I've had thirty-six calls already – and our mailing list figures have gone through the roof.
Margaret: What is our next show?
Gordon: Does it matter? They love us.
Joyce: Oh, Gordon. We've wronged you.
Gordon: Forget it, Joyce. That's show biz.
Bernard: Gordon, I'd like to shake your hand.
Gordon: Yes, I bet you would, Bernard.
Margaret: So it's not all over for Little Grimley?
Gordon: It's never over, Margaret, until the...

Gordon stops and turns to look at Joyce, who has quietly started singing "There's no business like show business". Her delivery has the very slow, but very determined feel of an anthem, and it's quite moving. The others exchange glances and, one by one, they join in - first Bernard, then Margaret and finally Gordon - as the song gains energy, volume and pace. At its climax, all four are on their feet, singing their hearts out, as a single spotlight encloses them. They finish the song with a magnificent flourish, the spotlight cuts to black. Curtain.